Introduction

With so many health benefits, it's no wonder fermented foods are on the top of everyone's list of must eat food. Fermented foods are an excellent way to get vitamins and minerals that are essential to good health. These vitamins and minerals include; b-vitamins, pro-biotics, and omega 3 fatty acids. B-vitamins provide the body with what it needs for a healthy immune system and energy, and omega 3 fatty acids provide the body with good fats that help to preserve healthy function of the circulatory system.

Pro-biotics are essential to a healthy digestive system. These good bacteria help with the breakdown of foods and aid in the proper absorption of the nutrients. Pro-biotics are present in Lacto-fermentation; when you eat yogurt or other foods produced through Lacto-fermentation you ingest pro-biotics and they colonize your gut and work their magic.

Fermentation and its health benefits can come only from food that has not been pasteurized or heated to high temperatures to destroy bacteria. This becomes a dilemma for those who want the health benefits provided by the live bacteria. The only way to be sure your fermented foods have these health benefits is to do the fermenting yourself. However, yogurt and kefir products still deliver if they contain "live cultures."

You are probably thinking that all of this fermentation stuff is useless if you cannot purchase the items in a store. This is not true! Fermentation at home is easy, really easy! Once you learn how to ferment your own food, you will gain all of the health benefits without any of the not-so-good stuff like increased sodium or added sugars.

Learning to ferment your own food and drink items is not as difficult as you may think. There are recipes for fermented food dishes from around the world; almost every culture has fermented foods, drinks, and recipes to call their own. Your new fermenting skills are going to open up a whole world of tastes and textures you didn't know existed.

There is evidence that Paleo-Americans, the first people to cross the Beringia land bridge at the Bering Strait, relied on fermentation to keep their food edible. Eating a Paleo diet is a growing trend among health enthusiasts, and this diet includes fermented food. The Paleo diet, also known as a Stone Age diet, is made up of food that was available to hunter-gathers of the Paleolithic era.

Growing interest in fermented foods is fueled by research into the microbiota of the human digestive tract. Some evidence suggests that good bacteria, such as lactobacillus, aid the digestive tract in digesting and absorbing minerals and vitamins. The research also hints that adding just a few fermented foods or drinks to your regular diet can actually make you healthier.

This book is full of fermented recipes. Anything listed in the ingredients can be found in most health food stores. You can even purchase starter kits for making yogurt and other foods that use lactobacillus. You don't really need any special skills or knowledge to ferment your own food at home. You don't need to purchase any kitchen appliances or special pots, a few glass jugs and different sized Mason jars is all you will use.

The process you will learn is known as lacto-fermentation, which relies on lactobacillus. Lactobacillus consumes sugar in the fermentation process. Salt is necessary too, but you can control how much you use. The results of fermenting your own food depend largely on your taste. Once you are used to creating the food in the recipes, you will be able to taste the mixture while it ferments and stop the fermentation process when you are satisfied with the taste.

Fermented desserts require a few more steps than veggie or fruit fermentation, but they really taste great. You can even make your own cheese from nuts and fermentation! It takes a bit of time to produce cheese from nuts, but it is worth every second. Everything from cheesecake to chocolate treats can be prepared through fermentation.

Chapter 1 - Fermentation and Your Health

Research on fermented food has increased in recent years and the newest findings point to various positive benefits for health. You will probably be surprised to learn that fermentation has been around for more than a millennium; it has long been used to keep food fresh. Today we know that fermentation has many health benefits. According to new studies, fermentation can enhance the nutritional component of foods by increasing the bioavailability of minerals and adding vitamin content.

Almost everyone is familiar with the health benefits of yogurt, which is a fermented dairy food. Actually, most people are familiar with a slew of fermented foods: pickles, sauerkraut, kimchi, yogurt, and cheese, to name just a few. Fermentation is also used in making wine, beer, and other alcoholic beverages. The more we learn about fermented foods and drinks, the more health benefits we discover. Today there is a lot of discussion about the benefits of fermented food for weight loss, digestive health, and even allergies.

The simplest reason that fermentation has so many benefits is that it is generated by a process involving living organisms that can change sugar into gasses, alcohol, and acids. Fermentation changes the original organic matter and, in the process, it changes the way our body interacts with the food and absorbs the nutrients. Probiotics are found in live yogurt cultures and kefir; the yogurt is said to be live because yeast is "alive."

There are many digestive health benefits associated with fermented food. Evidence for the effectiveness of fermented food on digestive health is still being gathered, but the early data is promising. The bacteria in fermented food predigest the food. That is what fermentation is all about: The predigested food is easier for our stomachs to digest, and the nutrients are more readily absorbed. Friendly probiotic bacteria actually keep us regular by replacing probiotics lost because of antibiotic use.

Another interesting fact is that fermentation in the production of kimchi and sauerkraut increases levels of glucosinolate, which has been identified as a possible cancer fighter. There is still more research to be done, but the initial results are promising. Introducing good bacteria into our bodies through eating fermented foods may even reduce swelling and provide relief for auto-immune conditions.

The human immune system responds to the health of the digestive tract. Immunity can be improved by traditional treatments, but fermented foods can also do the job. The bacteria in fermented food eventually take up residence in the digestive tract and, each time you ingest fermented food, it replenishes this colony of helpful bacteria. These micro-organisms speed absorption of many key nutrients that boost immunity. This fast and easy absorption means that the nutrients are released to the body more quickly.

The human digestive tract is very hostile to foreign microbes. The growing interest in fermented food and its purported health benefits has led to research to prove or disprove the claims that these microbes make it through the upper GI tract alive. If any benefits are to be seen, the microbes in the fermented food need to withstand these hostile conditions in order to end up in the lower GI, where they need to be. The testing and research showed that, against all odds, these microbes do survive the upper GI tract. They also survive in the lower GI tract in large numbers!

How much is too much fermented food? If you are consuming fermented foods for health, is it possible to consume too much? No, most research shows that you cannot consume too much, or so much that the probiotics become a problem. As with any food, you should always eat a healthy balanced diet, and that should include fermented foods.

Introducing fermented food into your diet will produce symptoms because the microbes are working to heal your digestive tract. The most common symptoms are bloating, loose stool, gas, or constipation. These symptoms should show up early and lessen over a few days as your body adjusts. If they last longer or disrupt your day, you should remove the fermented food from your diet, wait for the symptoms to pass, and then begin again.

The recipes in this book encompass a wide variety of foods, drinks, and even condiments. If you are adding as much as you can to your diet, you may want to consider the salt and or sugar content. These recipes do not contain enormous amounts of salt or sugar, but eating too much of anything is never beneficial. If you are unhappy with the salt or sugar content, you can alter it.

Altering the salt or sugar content in a fermented recipe is fine as long as you do not remove too much of either. Lactobacillus requires sugar to ferment and salt keeps the bad microbes from invading and taking over your ferment. Use caution when lowering the amount of these ingredients in your recipes.

Almost every veggie and fruit can be fermented. You can use the recipes in this book to create your own, based on your palate. Basic fermenting occurs as long as you add what you need to begin the process. Replacing a veggie or fruit in your recipe will not change the fermentation ingredients. Experiment and find what works best for you.

Chapter 2 – Fermented Food Recipes

All of these recipes are great as side dishes, some are condiments to compliment your meal, and still others could be considered a main dish. As you try each recipe, take notes on which ones you enjoy the most and what foods they go well with. Everyone knows sauerkraut is great on a hot dog, but is it a good complement to chicken or beef? Everyone's tastes are different and what is delicious to some may not be delicious to others. You will eventually become good at pairing your fermented recipes with other foods to create awesome meals that are healthy and taste great.

Lacto-fermentation is the best way to ferment foods at home. This type of fermentation relies on lactobacillus bacteria; this type of bacterium feeds on sugar and the byproduct is lactic acid. Almost any fruit or vegetable can be fermented using this method at home, but there are a few guidelines you should follow to ensure that your fermented foods turn out perfect and healthy.

Guidelines for Lacto-Fermenting Food at Home

You will need a few basic instruments for fermenting your own foods at home. A good glass vessel is important for fermenting. Some may suggest ceramic or other types of pots or vessels, but glass allows you to see the food and this can help you determine if you need to add water or remove any film that may form. White film on top of your fermenting food is a type of mold; this mold can be removed without any harm to the fermenting process.

If you plan to make several different fermented items, you may want to get yourself some Mason jars. Mason jars come in a variety of sizes and they have lids. During the fermenting process you need to cover the food, so a lid is a big plus. If you plan to make a large quantity of a single recipe, a large glass container with a lid is your best choice.

There are a few different ways to start off your fermentation. You can use a fermentation starter, which is available from many different organic or health food stores. A fermentation starter provides the lactobacillus bacteria but this bacterium is also present on your food and salt stops other bacteria from multiplying. Some people use seaweed for fermenting because it contains enough salt/sodium to protect the food from bad bacteria while allowing the lactobacillus to multiply.

Salt is necessary for fermenting because it keeps the bad bacteria in check. A good rule to follow is 3 tablespoons per 5 pounds of vegetables. You can adjust the salt content of your fermentation recipes to suit your taste, but some salt is needed. Here is a list of other herbs that can be added to your fermentation recipe to add flavor and spice.

- Bay Leaves
- Dill
- Garlic
- Cinnamon Sticks
- Coriander Seeds
- Whole Peppercorn
- Whole Cloves
- Mustard Seeds

When one of these spices or herbs is called for in a recipe, it will be listed with the amount to use. If you decide to branch out and create your own recipes, this list will come in handy. Try using your favorite spices and herbs even if they are not listed here because you may like the outcome.

Lacto-fermentation occurs naturally once the fruit or vegetable is cut up or shredded and placed in the jar with water and salt. The liquid must cover all of the food so mold will not grow on top and the fermentation is even. The recipes in this section will produce a gallon of fermented food. Make sure the lid is closed and put the jar on a towel to absorb any liquid that may leak when fermentation begins.

Apple and Juniper Berry Sauerkraut

Serving Size: ½ cup

Calories: 22.4

Fat: 0.2 g - 0.3%

Saturated Fat: 0.0 g - 0.2%

Trans Fat: 0.0 g

Cholesterol: 0.0 mg - 0.0%

Sodium: 780 mg - 32.5%

Total Carbohydrates: 5.1 g - 1.7%

Dietary Fiber: 3.1 g - 12.5%

Sugars: 1.9 g

Protein: 1.1 g - 2.1%

Ingredients

3 heads of shredded cabbage

2 peeled and chopped apples

3 tablespoons of caraway seeds

3 tablespoons of crushed juniper berries

¼ cup of salt/sea salt

Instructions

Combine all of the ingredients except the salt and put the mixture in your fermentation jar. Do it in layers: Add a little mixture and a little salt, squish it to release the juice/water from the cabbage and apples, and repeat until the mixture is all gone. Fill the gallon jar and leave an inch at the top for expansion during fermentation. If there is not enough juice/water to cover the food completely, add 4 cups of water for each 2 tablespoons of salt. Make sure the food is completely covered by the brine and close the lid.

Place your covered jar in a warm place and let it sit for at least 7 days. Check the sauerkraut periodically while it is fermenting to make sure the liquid still covers the food completely. Taste after 7 days and, if you are satisfied with the taste, move it to the refrigerator to stop the fermentation process.

Lacto-Fermented Pickles/Sour Pickles

Serving Size: 1 pickle

Calories: 4.3

Fat: 0.1 g - 0.1%

Saturated Fat: 0.0 g - 0.1%

Trans Fat: 0.0 g

Cholesterol: 0.0 mg - 0.0%

Sodium: 468 mg - 19.5%

Total Carbohydrates: 0.9 g - 0.3%

Dietary Fiber: 0.5 g - 1.9%

Sugars: 0.4 g

Protein: 0.1 g - 0.3%

Ingredients

1 gallon of pickling cucumber without a wax coating

2 fresh dill bunches

16 whole, peeled garlic cloves

3 tablespoons of peppercorn

3 tablespoons of mustard seeds

3 tablespoons of cloves

3 tablespoons of bay leaves

5 tablespoons of salt/sea salt

Instructions

Soak for at least 4 hours, then scrub the cucumbers.

Put the cucumbers into the jar a few at a time and add the spices, garlic, and dill in between as you go.

Make a brine by mixing - 8 cups of water with 5 tablespoons of salt/sea salt. Make sure all of the salt dissolves in the water, then pour it over the cucumbers and spices in your jar. Make sure the food is completely covered in brine before closing the lid.

Let the cucumbers ferment for at least 5 days, then taste them and, if they need more fermentation, leave them and taste them periodically up to a maximum of 10 days. Put the jar in the refrigerator to stop the fermentation and enjoy.

Beet Kavas

Serving Size: 1 cup

Calories: 73.8

Fat: 0.1 g - 0.1%

Saturated Fat: 0.0 g - 0.1%

Trans Fat: 0.0 g

Cholesterol: 0.0 mg - 0.0%

Sodium: 300 mg - 12.5%

Total Carbohydrates: 18.5 g - 6.2%

Dietary Fiber: 3.0 g - 11.8%

Sugars: 15.4 g

Protein: 0.9 g - 1.8%

Ingredients

4 peeled and chopped large beets

5 tablespoons of salt/sea salt

Instructions

Mix the salt and the beets together and put the mix in your jar. Add water to the jar until the food is completely covered and mix well to dissolve the salt.

Place the jar in a warm place and allow it to ferment for 2 days, then place it in the refrigerator to stop the fermentation process and enjoy.

Beet kavas juice can be used in place of vinegar in salads along with the beets!

Peach Chutney

Serving Size: 1 cup

Calories: 110.0

Fat: 0.1 g - 0.1%

Saturated Fat: 0.0 g - 0.0%

Trans Fat: 0.0 g

Cholesterol: 0.0 mg - 0.0%

Sodium: 10 mg - 0.4%

Total Carbohydrates: 28.9 g - 9.6%

Dietary Fiber: 3.3 g - 13.0%

Sugars: 25.7 g

Protein: 1.6 g - 3.2%

Ingredients

16 chopped-up peaches

1 ½ cups of raisins

1 ½ cups of chopped-up pecans

2 tablespoons of salt/sea salt

Juice of 5 lemons

4 finely chopped onions

4 tablespoons of grated ginger

4 dried or fresh chopped-up hot peppers

Instructions

In a large bowl, mix all of the ingredients together. Put the mixture into your jar and squish it by pounding: The point is to squeeze out the juices to create a liquid that will cover the mixture completely. If you need more liquid, mix 2 tablespoons of salt with 4 cups of water, stir until the salt dissolves and add this to the jar to cover the mixture.

Place the jar in a warm place and allow it to ferment for at least 2 days. Check the taste after 2 days. If you are satisfied, move it into the refrigerator; if you think it needs to ferment more, you can leave it for another 2 days, 4 days total, before putting it into the fridge.

Fruit and Veggie Combo

Serving Size: 1 cup

Calories: 296.5

Calories from Fat: 20 g

Fat: 2.2 g - 3.4%

Saturated Fat: 0.4 g - 1.8%

Trans Fat: 0.0 g

Cholesterol: 0.0 mg - 0.0%

Sodium: 1291 mg - 53.8%

Total Carbohydrates: 65.3 g - 21.8%

Dietary Fiber: 3.7 g - 14.7%

Sugars: 58.5 g

Protein: 3.7 g - 7.3%

Ingredients

4 peeled and diced carrots

4 peeled and diced apples

4 cups of cauliflower

2 ½ tablespoons of ginger

6 thinly sliced green onions

6 tablespoons of salt/sea salt

Instructions

Put all of the vegetables and fruit in a large bowl, add the ginger, and mix it well with your hands.

Put the mixture into your jar a little bit at a time with some of the salt and squish it and pound it up to release the liquid in the food. If the liquid you create does not cover the mixture completely, add 2 tablespoons of salt to 4 cups of water and mix well to dissolve the salt. Then pour the salt water over the mixture, leaving at least 1 inch between the mixture and the lid.

Close the lid, put the jar in a warm place, and allow it to ferment for at least 3 days, with a maximum of 5 days. Taste it periodically; once you are satisfied with the taste, pit it in the refrigerator to stop the fermenting process and enjoy.

Fermented Salsa

Serving Size: – 1 cup

Calories: 43.3

Calories from Fat: 5 g

Fat: 0.5 g - 0.8%

Saturated Fat: 0.1 g - 0.3%

Trans Fat: 0.0 g

Cholesterol: 0.0 mg - 0.0%

Sodium: 16 mg - 0.6%

Total Carbohydrates: 9.6 g - 3.2%

Dietary Fiber: 2.6 g - 10.2%

Sugars: 0.0 g

Protein: 1.7 g - 3.4%

Ingredients

12 cups of chopped-up tomatoes

2 seeded and chopped cups of jalapenos

¼ cup of dried oregano

2 tablespoons of cumin

6 chopped garlic cloves

2 chopped onions

¼ cup of salt/sea salt

Instructions

Wear gloves; jalapenos can irritate the skin. Mix all of the ingredients together in a large bowl.

Little by little, put the mixture into the jar and squash it down to release the liquid, adding salt as you go. If you do not have enough extracted liquid to cover the salsa, mix 2 tablespoons of salt with 4 cups of water and mix until the salt dissolves, then pour it over your salsa until it is completely covered and there is 1 inch between the salsa and the lid.

Close the lid, put the jar in a warm place, and let it ferment for at least 3 days, with a maximum of 5 days. Check the taste after 3 days; if you are satisfied, put the salsa in the refrigerator to stop fermentation. If you think it needs more time, leave it and check it until you are satisfied, but leave it no longer than 5 days.

Fermented Cauliflower

Serving Size: 1 cup

Calories: 11.8

Calories from Fat: 1 g

Fat: 0.1 g - 0.1%

Saturated Fat: 0.0 g - 0.0%

Trans Fat: 0.0 g

Cholesterol: 0.0 mg - 0.0%

Sodium: 5 mg - 0.2%

Total Carbohydrates: 2.7 g - 0.9%

Dietary Fiber: 0.5 g - 2.2%

Sugars: 2.1 g

Protein: 0.4 g - 0.8%

Ingredients

2 heads of cauliflower

4 large jalapenos cleaned of seeds and minced

1 ½ teaspoons of salt

Instructions

Wash and slice the cauliflower heads thinly, about ⅛ inch thick.

Wash and clean the seeds from the jalapenos and dice them.

Place the veggies in a bowl and add the salt, then toss and mix the veggies so the salt is dispersed throughout.

Put the mixture into your container and smoosh it with your fists, compressing the veggies and releasing the liquid. If the liquid you gather does not cover the veggies in the container, add ½ teaspoon of salt to ½ cup of water and pour over the mix until the veggies are completely covered.

Put the cover on the container and set it aside in a warm place for at least one week, up to a maximum of 3 weeks. Taste the mix periodically after a week and, when you are satisfied, place the container in the refrigerator and enjoy.

Red Kimchi

Serving Size: ½ cup

Calories: 22.5

Calories from Fat: 1 g

Fat: 0.1 g - 0.1%

Saturated Fat: 0.0 g - 0.0%

Trans Fat: 0.0 g

Cholesterol: 0.0 mg - 0.0%

Sodium: 208 mg - 8.7%

Total Carbohydrates: 4.3 g - 1.4%

Dietary Fiber: 2.3 g - 9.3%

Sugars: 1.0 g

Protein: 1.2 g - 2.4%

Ingredients

3 pounds of red cabbage

8 ounces of radish (daikon is best)

1 ½ tablespoon of salt

2 tablespoons of ginger

¼ cup of red pepper flakes

2 cloves of garlic

1 teaspoon of turmeric powder

1/3 of a medium onion

Instructions

Clean and slice the cabbage and radish, then toss then together with the salt in a bowl.

Mince the onion and the garlic cloves and combine them with the spices to make a paste.

After letting the cabbage and radish sit for a while, mix with the spice paste, making sure that the paste is distributed evenly, and put it all into your fermentation jar. Press and squish the mix to extract liquid. If you cannot press enough liquid from the cabbage mixture, you can add ½ cup of water with ½ teaspoon of salt.

Close the container and leave it to ferment for at least 1 week, up to a maximum of 3 weeks depending on your tastes. Once you are satisfied, refrigerate to stop the fermentation process.

Sour Cream

Serving Size: 1 tablespoon

Calories: 23.2

Calories from Fat: 21 g

Fat: 2.4 g - 3.6%

Saturated Fat: 1.4 g - 6.9%

Trans Fat: 0.1 g

Cholesterol: 6.2 mg - 2.1%

Sodium: 10 mg - 0.4%

Total Carbohydrates: 0.3 g - 0.1%

Dietary Fiber: 0.0 g - 0.0%

Sugars: 0.3 g

Protein: 0.2 g - 0.5%

Ingredients

1 pack of sour cream starter (you can purchase sour cream starter packs in health food stores)

4 quarts of heavy cream

Instructions

Pour the heavy cream into a saucepan and heat until it reaches 145 degrees; use a thermometer and hold the temperature for 45 minutes, then cool the cream down to 77 degrees.

Add the packet of sour cream starter to the cooled cream and stir until the starter powder is completely dissolved.

Place the mixture in a jar; a large Mason jar is perfect. Cover with a paper towel and secure it with a rubber band. Place the jar in a warm dark area and allow the cream to ferment for 16 hours, then check the texture and taste. If the texture and taste are what you want, close the lid and place the sour cream in the refrigerator. This sour cream will stay fresh for 2-3 weeks.

Fermented Mayonnaise

Serving Size: 1 Tablespoon

Calories: 48.6

Calories from Fat: 45 g

Fat: 5.0 g - 7.6%

Saturated Fat: 0.8 g - 3.9%

Trans Fat: 0.0 g

Cholesterol: 5.3 mg - 1.8%

Sodium: 101 mg - 4.2%

Total Carbohydrates: 1.2 g - 0.4%

Dietary Fiber: 0.0 g - 0.0%

Sugars: 0.7 g

Protein: 0.1 g - 0.3%

Ingredients
2 egg yolks

2 tablespoons of lemon juice

1 cup of olive oil

Salt and pepper

¼ teaspoon of mustard powder

1 tablespoon of whey

Instructions

Fill a small bowl with water and let it sit for 2 minutes, dump the water and dry it completely.

Put the egg yolks and lemon juice into the bowl and whisk until completely blended.

Begin adding the olive oil very slowly, whisking as you add it; continue whisking until the ingredients are well blended and the mixture is thick and creamy.

Now add the rest of the ingredients and salt and pepper according to your own taste.

Put a cover over the bowl and leave it to ferment for 8 hours, then move it to the refrigerator. It will be good for up to 2 weeks.

Bulgur Wheat Pancakes with Cinnamon Honey Syrup

Serving Size: ½ cup

Calories: 220.0

Calories from Fat: 14 g

Fat: 1.5 g - 2.3%

Saturated Fat: 0.5 g - 2.5%

Trans Fat: 0.0 g

Cholesterol: 5.0 mg - 1.7%

Sodium: 520 mg - 21.7%

Total Carbohydrates: 42.0 g - 14.0%

Dietary Fiber: 4.0 g - 16.0%

Sugars: 6.0 g

Protein: 8.0 g - 16.0%

Ingredients

2 cups of bulgur wheat flour

2 cups of cultured buttermilk

1 teaspoon of salt or sea salt

2 teaspoons of baking powder

2 eggs

2 tablespoons of olive oil

1 teaspoon of vanilla

2 teaspoons of cinnamon

½ cup of honey

½ cup of butter

2 teaspoons of cinnamon

Instructions

Stir together the flour and the buttermilk and let the mixture sit overnight.

Mix in the salt, eggs, baking powder, oil, vanilla, flour, and cinnamon, then mix it all into the flour and buttermilk; blend well but do not over-stir.

Cook the pancakes in a hot skillet until both sides are a golden brown color.

While waiting for the pancakes to finish, make the cinnamon honey syrup. Heat the butter, honey, and cinnamon, then stir until completely blended

Cover the pancakes with the warm syrup and serve.

Tasty Tarragon Chicken Salad

Serving Size: One scoop

Calories: 140.0

Calories from Fat: 27 g

Fat: 3.0 g - 4.6%

Saturated Fat: 1.0 g - 5.0%

Trans Fat: 0.0 g

Cholesterol: 45.0 mg - 15.0%

Sodium: 800 mg - 33.3%

Total Carbohydrates: 12.0 g - 4.0%

Dietary Fiber: 3.0 g - 12.0%

Sugars: 2.0 g

Protein: 16.0 g - 32.0%

Ingredients

4 cups of cooked chicken, chopped up

¼ cup of green onions sliced

½ cup of chopped celery

½ cup of dried sunflower seeds, soaked

2/3 cup of fermented mayonnaise

½ tablespoon of Dijon mustard

2 tablespoons of lemon juice

1 teaspoon of sea salt

2 tablespoons of fresh chopped tarragon and 2 teaspoons of dried tarragon

Instructions

In a large bowl, mix the chicken with the tarragon, onion, celery, and sunflower seeds.

In another bowl, mix the mayonnaise, lemon juice, salt, and Dijon mustard, and whisk until well blended.

Pour the mayonnaise mixture over the chicken and other ingredients; mix until well blended, then refrigerate before serving.

Chapter 3 – Fermented Drink Recipes

Basic Beverage Fermentation

The basic fermentation method for making a beverage that can hydrate you much better than water can is simple. This recipe can be used to create hundreds of delicious, good-for-you drinks. You can experiment with this and you will discover tastes you love.

The basic recipe for any mineral- and vitamin-rich fermented drink is as follows:

½ cup of whey – this can be drained from plain yogurt; pour off the liquid without mixing the yogurt. The liquid you poured out is whey; or you can purchase whey in a health food store.

1 gallon of filtered or spring water

Sweeteners and flavoring – add juices or even pureed fruit!

That's it; let it sit in a warm dark place for 2-4 days, taste it and, if you are satisfied with the taste, put it into the refrigerator and enjoy.

Probiotic Lemonade

Serving Size: 1 glass

Calories: 71.5

Calories from Fat: 2 g

Fat: 0.3 g - 0.4%

Saturated Fat: 0.0 g - 0.0%

Trans Fat: 0.0 g

Cholesterol: 0.0 mg - 0.0%

Sodium: 3 mg - 0.1%

Total Carbohydrates: 18.2 g - 6.1%

Dietary Fiber: 0.1 g - 0.4%

Sugars: 16.2 g

Protein: 0.1 g - 0.2%

Ingredients

6 squeezed lemons

½ cup of sugar

½ cup of whey (you can use the liquid drained from plain yogurt, as described above)

Spring water

Instructions

Put all of the ingredients, including 3-4 cups of spring water, into a ½-gallon jug. Mix and stir the liquid until the sugar dissolves, then fill the jug with spring water, leaving an inch at the top between the lemonade and the lid, and stir.

Leave the lemonade to ferment for at least 2 days. The longer you let it ferment, the tangier/tarter it becomes. Once you are satisfied with the taste, put the jug into the refrigerator and enjoy.

Fermented Orange Juice

Serving Size: 8 oz.

Calories: 109.6

Calories from Fat: 3 g

Fat: 0.3 g - 0.5%

Saturated Fat: 0.0 g - 0.2%

Trans Fat: 0.0 g

Cholesterol: 0.0 mg - 0.0%

Sodium: 2 mg - 0.1%

Total Carbohydrates: 25.4 g - 8.5%

Dietary Fiber: 0.5 g - 2.0%

Sugars: 0.0 g

Protein: 2.0 g - 4.0%

Ingredients

2 ½ cups of freshly squeezed orange juice

2 tablespoons of whey (you can use the liquid drained from plain yogurt, as described above)

1 cup of spring or filtered water

Some/pinch sea salt

Instructions

Put all of the ingredients into a quart-sized jug or Mason jar, leaving at least an inch of space at the top of the jar. Close the lid and shake the mixture vigorously, then let it sit and ferment for 2 days. Put the OJ in the fridge and enjoy.

Forever Kombucha

Serving Size: 8 oz.

Calories: 90.0

Calories from Fat: 0 g

Fat: 0.0 g - 0.0%

Saturated Fat: 0.0 g - 0.0%

Trans Fat: 0.0 g

Cholesterol: 0.0 mg - 0.0%

Sodium: 10 mg - 0.4%

Total Carbohydrates: 24.0 g - 8.0%

Dietary Fiber: 0.0 g - 0.0%

Sugars: 23.0 g

Protein: 0.0 g - 0.0%

This kombucha recipe produces a never-ending supply. You simply draw off kombucha from the top and add an equal amount of sweet tea to replace it. Once you draw off some kombucha, you can put it in bottle/container you can shake, add ¼ cup of sweet tea, shake it up and put it in the refrigerator and enjoy.

Ingredients

2 tablespoons of loose tea (without the bag)

1 cup of sugar

1 kombucha starter (this is a starter culture for kombucha that can be found in most health food stores)

1 cup of kombucha tea (this can be purchased in health food stores)

Instructions

Boil 1 quart of water, remove from the heat, then add the loose tea and sugar. Stir until the sugar is completely dissolved and let the tea sit until it is at room temperature.

Strain the loose tea from the water into the container you are going to use for the forever kombucha; a gallon jug should do. Now add 3 quarts of water, the starter, and the kombucha tea to the jug. Cover the jug and let it ferment for a week.

After a week you can draw off about 25% of the kombucha tea and put it in your shakable container. Then replace what you took with sweet tea. You can continue this process of drawing off and replacing up to 3 times a week.

Add sweet tea to the container with you portion of kombucha tea, shake well and refrigerate.

Hydrating Dehydrated Water Kefir Grains

If the water kefir grains you have purchased are dry or dehydrated, you will have to re-hydrate them before making the water kefir.

Ingredients

Dehydrated water kefir grains

¼ cup of sugar

3-4 cups of filtered or spring water

Instructions

Boil the water, let it cool a bit, then pour it into a glass jar; a large Mason jar is perfect for this. Put the sugar into the jar with the water and stir with a wooden or plastic utensil until the sugar granules are completely dissolved. Leave the sugar water to cool to room temperature.

Dump your packet of water kefir grains into the sugar water, then cover with a paper towel and use a rubber band to hold the paper towel to the jar. Now place it in a warm dark place for 3-4 days.

After 3 days, check the kefir grains. Once they are swollen and translucent, they are ready to be used in your water kefir recipe.

Water Kefir

Serving Size: 8 oz.

Calories: 149.1

Calories from Fat: 73 g

Fat: 8.2 g - 12.5%

Saturated Fat: 0.0 g - 0.0%

Trans Fat: 0.0 g

Cholesterol: 0.0 mg - 0.0%

Sodium: 107 mg - 4.5%

Total Carbohydrates: 11.2 g - 3.7%

Dietary Fiber: 0.0 g - 0.0%

Sugars: 11.2 g

Protein: 7.7 g - 15.4%

Ingredients

½ cup of sugar

½ cup of water

3 cups of room temperature water

Water kefir grains, hydrated

Instructions

Pour ½ cup of water into the jar or jug and add ½ cup of hot water.

Stir the mixture with a wooden or plastic utensil until the sugar dissolves completely.

Dump in the water kefir grains, cover the jar or jug, and place it in a warm dark place for 24-48 hours.

Place the water kefir in the refrigerator and enjoy.

Keep the Kefir Going

Strain the kefir grains from your water kefir.

Place the kefir grains in a new batch of sugar water, then ferment as you did for the first batch.

You can do this over and over and keep you and your family supplied with fresh kefir water right from your own refrigerator.

Coconut Water Kefir

Serving Size: 8 oz.

Calories: 156

Calories from Fat: 73 g

Fat: 8.2 g - 12.5%

Saturated Fat: 0.0 g - 0.0%

Trans Fat: 0.0 g

Cholesterol: 0.0 mg - 0.0%

Sodium: 107 mg - 4.5%

Total Carbohydrates: 11.2 g - 3.7%

Dietary Fiber: 0.0 g - 0.0%

Sugars: 11.2 g

Protein: 7.7 g - 15.4%

Ingredients

1 quart of coconut water

3 tablespoons of hydrated water kefir grains

Optional: add pureed fruit to the coconut water kefir

Instructions

Put the kefir grains into the coconut water and cover with a paper towel and rubber band.

Place the mixture in a warm dark place for 24-48 hours, then remove the kefir grains. If you are adding the fruit, puree the fruit and the fermented coconut kefir water together.

Place the water in the refrigerator and enjoy.

Hydrating Milk Kefir Grains

If you have dehydrated milk kefir grains, you will have to activate them as you did with the water kefir grains before you can make milk kefir

Ingredients

One packet of milk kefir grains (makes about 4 cups of hydrated milk kefir grains)

Pasteurized milk

Instructions

Empty the dehydrated milk kefir grains into a jar or jug, cover it with a paper towel, and secure the towel with a rubber band.

Place in a warm dark place for 8- 24 hours; begin checking the milk after about 23 hours, then check every hour for changes in the milk. Once you notice a change in the milk to a thicker texture, drain out the kefir grains, put them into a fresh jar of milk, and add an extra ½ cup of milk.

Place in a warm place and do as you did before: After 23 hours, begin checking the mild for texture changes. Check the milk and strain the grains, then place them in fresh milk, plus ½ cup until the total amount of milk is about 4 cups. The kefir grains are activated and you can use them in the milk kefir recipe

Milk Kefir

Serving Size: 8 oz.

Calories: 210.0

Calories from Fat: 72 g

Fat: 8.0 g - 12.3%

Saturated Fat: 6.0 g - 30.0%

Trans Fat: 0.0 g

Cholesterol: 35.0 mg - 11.7%

Sodium: 120 mg - 5.0%

Total Carbohydrates: 25.0 g - 8.3%

Dietary Fiber: 1.0 g - 4.0%

Sugars: 24.0 g

Protein: 7.0 g - 14.0%

Ingredients

1-2 teaspoons of activated milk kefir grains

Milk

Instructions

Pour the activated milk kefir grains into a jar or jug and fill it with fresh milk

Cover the jar with a paper towel, secure the towel with a rubber band, and put the jar in a warm dark place for 24 hours. The finished milk kefir should have a nice aroma. Strain the grains from the milk and place the milk in the refrigerator. Place the grains into the jar and add fresh milk for a new batch

Spiced Chai Milk Kefir

Serving Size: 8 oz.

Calories: 210.0

Calories from Fat: 72 g

Fat: 8.0 g - 12.3%

Saturated Fat: 6.0 g - 30.0%

Trans Fat: 0.0 g

Cholesterol: 35.0 mg - 11.7%

Sodium: 120 mg - 5.0%

Total Carbohydrates: 25.0 g - 8.3%

Dietary Fiber: 1.0 g - 4.0%

Sugars: 24.0 g

Protein: 7.0 g - 14.0%

Ingredients

2 cups of milk kefir

1 spiced chi tea bag

A bit of honey

Instructions

Pour the fermented milk kefir into a jar, add the spiced chi tea bag, and cover tightly with a lid. Place the mixture in a warm dark place for 12-24 hours, then remove the chi tea bag and add honey to taste. Keep in the refrigerator and enjoy.

Probiotic Smoothie

Serving Size: 8 oz.

Calories: 45.0

Calories from Fat: 0 g

Fat: 0.0 g - 0.0%

Saturated Fat: 0.0 g - 0.0%

Trans Fat: 0.0 g

Cholesterol: 0.0 mg - 0.0%

Sodium: 35 mg - 1.5%

Total Carbohydrates: 11.0 g - 3.7%

Dietary Fiber: 0.0 g - 0.0%

Sugars: 8.0 g

Protein: 1.0 g - 2.0%

Ingredients

4 cups of milk

12 whey ice cubes (drain the liquid from plain yogurt or purchase whey in a health food store, then pour the whey into ice cube trays and freeze)

Fresh fruit puree

Sweeten to taste

Instructions

Pour the 4 cups of milk, sugar or honey to taste, and whey ice cubes into the blender. Pulse the blender until the whey cubes are starting to break apart. Add the puree and blend until smooth.

You can add any flavoring to this smoothie, even vanilla and chocolate!

Chapter 4 – Fermented Dessert Recipes

Chocolate Sauerkraut Cake

Serving Size: 1 slice

Calories: 234.9

Calories from Fat: 94 g

Fat: 10.5 g - 16.1%

Saturated Fat: 3.1 g - 15.3%

Trans Fat: 0.0 g

Cholesterol: 26.9 mg - 9.0%

Sodium: 214 mg - 8.9%

Total Carbohydrates: 34.9 g - 11.6%

Dietary Fiber: 1.8 g - 7.2%

Sugars: 0.0 g

Protein: 2.6 g - 5.2%

Ingredients

¾ cup of sauerkraut, drained and chopped up

¾ cup of sugar

½ cup of honey

½ cup of butter

3 large eggs

1 teaspoon of vanilla

2 cups of flour

1 teaspoon of baking soda

1 teaspoon of baking powder

½ teaspoon of salt

1 cup of water

¾ cup of unsweetened cocoa powder

¾ cup of chopped-up walnuts

Instructions

Preheat the oven to 350 degrees F.

Using a sifter, sift all of the dry ingredients into a bowl and set aside. Now cream the sugar, vanilla, and butter together, add the honey and eggs, and beat until smooth.

Now add the powdered mix and water to the creamed mix, alternating between the powder and the water as you add them, then add the sauerkraut and mix well.

Grease two 9-inch pans and pour the batter into the pans evenly. Bake at 350 degrees F. for 30 minutes or until a toothpick that is inserted will come out clean.

Let cool completely before frosting.

Sweet Rice or Khao Mahk

Serving Size: 1 cup

Calories: 200.0

Calories from Fat: 32 g

Fat: 3.5 g - 5.4%

Saturated Fat: 0.0 g - 0.0%

Trans Fat: 0.0 g

Cholesterol: 0.0 mg - 0.0%

Sodium: 0 mg - 0.0%

Total Carbohydrates: 40.0 g - 13.3%

Dietary Fiber: 4.0 g - 16.0%

Sugars: 11.0 g

Protein: 3.0 g - 6.0%

This Thai dish begins with Thai sticky rice. Thai sticky rice is a special type of rice that has a sweet flavor when cooked.

Ingredients

4 cups and 2 tablespoons of sticky rice

½ cup of sugar

½ of one dried yeast ball (pound the ½ of yeast ball with a mortar and pestle until it is powder)

Instructions

Soak the sticky rice in warm water for at least 15 minutes, then rinse it in cold water until the water runs clear.

Steam the rice over medium heat for 30 minutes.

Dump the steamed rice onto a large baking sheet or tray and leave it to cool completely. Once it is cool, rinse the rice in cold water and use your hands to break up any rice that is stuck together and drain.

Put the rice in a large bowl and add the sugar. Using your hands, mix the rice and sugar well, being careful not to mash up or break the rice. Put the rice and sugar mixture into plastic bowls with covers, making sure the cover does not touch the rice; there should be at least an inch of room between the rice and the lid. Let the rice sit in the bowls outside of the refrigerator for 1-3 days, until you notice water coming from the rice and collecting at the bottom of the bowl. Once this happens, the Khao Mahk is done. Refrigerate and serve cold.

Fermented Cheese Cake

Serving Size: 1 slice

Calories: 257.6

Calories from Fat: 104 g

Fat: 11.6 g - 17.8%

Saturated Fat: 4.1 g - 20.5%

Trans Fat: 0.0 g

Cholesterol: 64.6 mg - 21.5%

Sodium: 258 mg - 10.7%

Total Carbohydrates: 33.7 g - 11.2%

Dietary Fiber: 0.8 g - 3.0%

Sugars: 0.0 g

Protein: 5.3 g - 10.6%

Ingredients

Filling

4 cups of cashews (softened in water for 4 hours)

2 cups of soaked pine nuts

¾ cup of virgin coconut oil (melted and cooled a bit)

¼ cup of honey raw

¼ cup of lemon juice (squeezed)

¼ cup + ⅛ cup of spring or filtered water

2 tablespoons of gelatin

2 teaspoons of vanilla

¼ teaspoon of salt/sea salt

¼ teaspoon of probiotic (can be purchased in health food stores)

Crust

2 ¼ cup of sprouted walnuts

¼ cup of extra virgin coconut oil (melted and cooled a bit)

½ teaspoon of cinnamon

Pinch of salt/sea salt

Instructions

Place the drained cashews and pine nuts, water, ½ cup of coconut oil, salt, and lemon juice in a blender and puree for 50 seconds.

Add the probiotic and puree for 10 seconds.

Pour all of the mixture into a large glass bowl or jar and press it down, making the top smooth and level.

Warm the remaining ¼ cup of coconut oil and pour it over the top of the puree in the container, make sure it goes from side to side, touching all sides of the glass to form a type of seal on the puree.

Cover the container lightly so air can get out. Mark the outside of the jar or bowl where the puree comes to.

Put the mixture in a warm dark place for at least 12 hours and no more than 1 ½ days. Keep it there until it rises and becomes porous.

Now take the fermented puree and dump it into a large bowl

Dissolve the gelatin in a ¼ cup of water of heat, stir until dissolved, and remove from heat. Cool a bit, then add the honey and stir.

Add the honey and gelatin mix to the fermented puree and fold it in.

Now make the crust.

Crust

Pulse the cashews in the blender until they are powdered. Add the remaining ingredients for the crust and pulse to combine. Do not over-pulse and create butter; it should be crumbly not a paste.

Press the crumbs into a spring form pan to create the crust.

Finish

Fill the spring form pan with the finished puree mixture/cheese cake filling and place in the refrigerator until it is firm enough to cut (at least overnight) then remove the spring form and enjoy

Chocolate Kefir Frozen Treats

Serving Size: 1 bar

Calories: 200.0

Calories from Fat: 63 g

Fat: 7.0 g - 10.8%

Saturated Fat: 6.0 g - 30.0%

Trans Fat: 0.0 g

Cholesterol: 35.0 mg - 11.7%

Sodium: 110 mg - 4.6%

Total Carbohydrates: 23.0 g - 7.7%

Dietary Fiber: 1.0 g - 4.0%

Sugars: 22.0 g

Protein: 7.0 g - 14.0%

Ingredients

1 cup of coconut milk kefir or plain milk kefir

3 tablespoons of unsweetened cocoa powder

3 tablespoons of sugar

½ teaspoon of vanilla

Pinch of sea salt

Instructions

Place all of the ingredients into the blender and blend until the mixture is smooth, then pour it into popsicle molds and freeze.

Orange Water Kefir Gelatin

Serving Size: 1 cup

Calories: 149.1

Calories from Fat: 73 g

Fat: 8.2 g - 12.5%

Saturated Fat: 0.0 g - 0.0%

Trans Fat: 0.0 g

Cholesterol: 0.0 mg - 0.0%

Sodium: 107 mg - 4.5%

Total Carbohydrates: 11.2 g - 3.7%

Dietary Fiber: 0.0 g - 0.0%

Sugars: 11.2 g

Protein: 7.7 g - 15.4%

Ingredients

3 cups of water kefir

1 cup of orange juice

4 tablespoons of honey or 3 tablespoons of sugar

5 tablespoons of gelatin powder

Instructions

Mix together 2 cups of water kefir, orange juice, and honey or sugar. Mix until the sugar is dissolved. Whisk the mixture and adjust the sugar or honey to taste.

Heat 1 cup of water kefir. Do not boil; heat it on a low flame and add the gelatin powder. Continue to mix and keep the heat low until the gelatin starts to dissolve, then remove from heat and whisk until the gelatin is completely dissolved.

When the gelatin is dissolved, add the juice-kefir mixture and mix well, then put it in the refrigerator for at least 4 hours to firm up and set.

Mascarpone Cheese

Serving Size: 1 Tablespoon

Calories: 120.0

Calories from Fat: 117 g

Fat: 13.0 g - 20.0%

Saturated Fat: 7.0 g - 35.0%

Trans Fat: 0.0 g

Cholesterol: 35.0 mg - 11.7%

Sodium: 15 mg - 0.6%

Total Carbohydrates: 0.0 g - 0.0%

Dietary Fiber: 0.0 g - 0.0%

Sugars: 0.0 g

Protein: 2.0 g - 4.0%

Ingredients

1 quart of half and half

2 tablespoons of lemon juice

Instructions

Use a double boiler to heat the half and half to 190 degrees; use a thermometer to avoid overheating the cream. Once it reaches 190, remove the cream from the heat and add the lemon juice, then whisk until it they are well blended

Let the cream sit for at least 5 minutes and stir occasionally until it thickens to a consistency that coats the spoon.

Put a colander over a bowl and spread butter muslin on the bottom of the colander. Pour the cream mixture into the colander and wait until the whey drains into the bowl. You can save this whey to use in other recipes. Let it drain for at least one hour

Put the mascarpone into an airtight container and store it in the refrigerator. It will thicken even more as it cools. For optimum flavor, serve as soon as it is cool. Mascarpone cheese will remain fresh for a week in the refrigerator

Mascarpone Fudge

Serving Size: 1 square

Calories: 130.0

Calories from Fat: 117 g

Fat: 13.0 g - 20.0%

Saturated Fat: 8.0 g - 40.0%

Trans Fat: 0.0 g

Cholesterol: 35.0 mg - 11.7%

Sodium: 15 mg - 0.6%

Total Carbohydrates: 3.0 g - 1.0%

Dietary Fiber: 0.0 g - 0.0%

Sugars: 3.0 g

Protein: 2.0 g - 4.0%

Ingredients

1 ½ pounds of semi-sweet chocolate chips

1 cup of mascarpone cheese

¼ cup of peanut butter

Chopped walnuts

Instructions

Grease an 8-inch glass baking dish with butter.

Melt the chocolate chips in a double boiler until smooth.

Add the mascarpone to the chips and whisk until completely blended.

Mix in the walnuts and peanut butter, stir until there is a blended swirl.

Move the fudge to the greased pan and smooth it until it has an even top.

Refrigerate for at least 12 hours, then cut and serve.

Autumn Sour Cream Spice Cake

Serving Size: 1 slice

Calories: 367.7

Calories from Fat: 105 g

Fat: 11.7 g - 18.0%

Saturated Fat: 3.2 g - 15.8%

Trans Fat: 0.0 g

Cholesterol: 49.9 mg - 16.6%

Sodium: 281 mg - 11.7%

Total Carbohydrates: 62.1 g - 20.7%

Dietary Fiber: 1.0 g - 4.1%

Sugars: 59.1 g

Protein: 4.5 g - 9.0%

Ingredients

2 cups of flour

1 ½ cups of brown sugar, packed

¾ teaspoon of ground cloves

1 teaspoon of ground cinnamon

½ teaspoon of nutmeg

1 ¼ teaspoon baking soda

1 teaspoon of baking powder

½ teaspoon of salt

1 cup of sour cream (recipe can be found in Chapter 2)

2 tablespoons of softened unsalted butter

¼ cup of butter flavored shortening

½ cup of water

2 large eggs

Instructions

Preheat the oven to 350 degrees, then grease and flour a 9 x 13-inch baking pan.

Mix the dry ingredients in a medium bowl.

In a larger bowl, whisk the remaining ingredients together until blended.

Fold the dry ingredients into the wet ingredients and whisk to blend; continue until the batter is completely blended.

Pour the batter into the greased and floured baking dish and bake for 30-35 minutes, depending on your oven.

Perfect Sourdough Peanut Butter Cookies

Serving Size: 2 Cookies

Calories: 71.6

Calories from Fat: 32 g

Fat: 3.5 g - 5.4%

Saturated Fat: 0.7 g - 3.4%

Trans Fat: 0.0 g

Cholesterol: 0.2 mg - 0.1%

Sodium: 62 mg - 2.6%

Total Carbohydrates: 8.8 g - 2.9%

Dietary Fiber: 0.3 g - 1.1%

Sugars: 4.8 g

Protein: 1.4 g - 2.9%

Ingredients

1 cup of starter (sourdough starter can be purchased in a health food store)

1 cup of peanut butter (organic is best)

1 cup of butter

2 eggs

1 cup of brown sugar

1 teaspoon of vanilla

2 cups of flour

1 teaspoon of baking soda

1 teaspoon of baking powder

½ teaspoon of sea salt or table salt

Instructions

Preheat the oven to 350 degrees.

Cream together the starter, peanut butter, butter, sugar, eggs, and vanilla.

In a different bowl, mix the flour, baking soda and powder and salt.

Blend the creamed ingredients and the dry ingredients together. The dough should have the right consistency for forming small balls; if it is too soft, add flour in small amounts until it has the right texture and consistency.

Roll the dough into small balls and place 2 inches apart on a greased cookie sheet.

Bake for 12-15 minutes, depending on your oven; the cookies are done when they begin to turn a light brown color.

Chocolate Cream Ice Cream

Serving Size: 1 scoop

Calories: 188.7

Calories from Fat: 113 g

Fat: 12.6 g - 19.3%

Saturated Fat: 7.7 g - 38.4%

Trans Fat: 0.0 g

Cholesterol: 44.4 mg - 14.8%

Sodium: 42 mg - 1.8%

Total Carbohydrates: 15.4 g - 5.1%

Dietary Fiber: 0.7 g - 2.7%

Sugars: 12.8 g

Protein: 3.5 g - 7.0%

Ingredients

½ pint of heavy cream

½ pint of sour cream